the whispers of God

j. elizabeth sharon

the whispers of God

j. elizabeth sharon

john 18:37c
press

Hardcover: 978-1-945505-35-5
Paperback: 978-1-945505-36-2
Kindle: 978-1-945505-37-9

Library of Congress Cataloging in Publication and LCCN on file with the
publisher.

Interior illustrations by J. Elizabeth Sharon
Publishing and production: Concierge Publishing Services, Omaha, Nebraska

Printed in the United States of America
10 9 8 7 6 5 4 3 2 1

dedication

i dedicate these words to the One
who gave them to me morning after
morning and also to the one whose
love guided me into the hands that
now hold my heart —Jesus Christ

"I'm thanking you, God, from a full heart,
I'm writing the book on your wonders, I'm whistling,
laughing, and jumping for joy.
I'm singing your song High God."

psalm 9:1-2
The Message

to think that david felt just like me
looking up at morningtide; the great big blue sea
letting oneself to be totally immersed
jumping, laughing, nothing rehearsed,
but rather moved by the awesomeness of God
like a child once again upon this sod
expressing in any way that i can
the very delight and wonder of man.

in 1998, He came to me…
as i sat journaling to Thee
He spoke and i wrote down His words –
and still to listen – taking down what i've heard.
so many years later, we continue to meet
morningtide, His company i keep
throughout the day He visits me
recording what is said by Thee
i offer to you —
hold out your hearts
hold out your minds
the eternal is speaking
to humankind

contents

sunrises

His glory proclaimed day in day out
silently no fanfare or shout
just as He rose from the grave
a quiet intention to be laid
resurrection His light to shine
to proclaim His life we find
the promise and His peace to reside
if in Him we abide —

sunrise 93

sapphire blue has come to embrace
my morningtide, His cloak of grace
that envelopes the dawn and also me
with His presence, His divine company
"awake My child and let me in –
be thou not troubled by what's within
let Me be your source of light
let Me guide you and give you sight"

sunrise 103

hello morning it's been too long
since i've witnessed the rise of dawn
even a couple of days away
is enough to make me say
i missed You.

sunrise 145

eagerly i watch as the night into day
a tender touch on the horizon displayed
from pitch, to purple and then a holy blue
one after another, so beautiful the hues,

laid upon the earth, bringing each into the day
the beauty of Your truth, as if to hear You say
" I AM with you" – no need to fear or fret
I AM goes before you – remember Me and let
Me lead the way –

"o Lord lead me in Your righteousness
because of my foes;
make Your way straight before me."

psalm 5:8

"I AM with you!"

sunrise 34

as i sit and watch the dawning appear
i am comforted, His illumination dear
whether the sky to brighten or in my mind
my understanding heightened and i to find
answers to questions i didn't even know i had
His light fills me with wonder often replacing the sad
with pearls of wisdom, evidence of light
and once again i'm given new sight –
as i sit and watch the dawning appear
i am comforted, His illumination dear
His silent beauty inside of me
portrayed by daybreak so all can see
i'm awed by its magnificence both inside and out
moved to worship, an audible shout
as i sit and watch the dawning appear
i am comforted, His illumination dear

sunrise 88

a light show of such magnitude on Christmas morn.
the skies full of lightening and thunder clouds worn –
announcing His birth in a most unconventional way –
yet why am i surprised, for it's His day!
and He doesn't do things expectantly
but rather, i believe rather exquisitely
this just another example – fireworks in the sky
with trumpet blast from above, sounding from on high
the wonder and excitement, even felt glee –
oh, how creative – my God is He

if i am a candle then there will be an end
to the light that i give, to the light i send
if i am the moon, only a reflection am i
of the light of the sun and the light to one's eye
if i am a lamp then there's oil to be poured
and when it runs out there will be light no more
if a chandelier, electricity is the power
that provides the light for a needed hour
but if a christian then Christ light to shine
for His is divine, perpetual and not mine

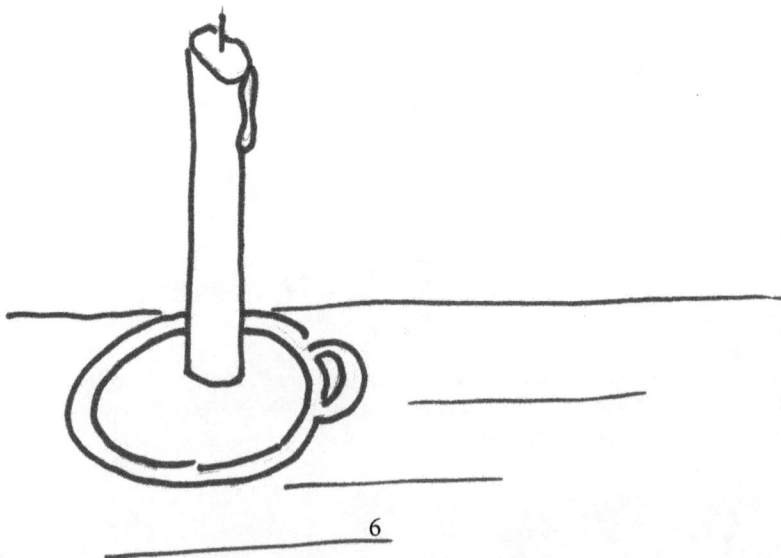

sunrise 4

ever so slight the pink laid upon each bough
a gentle kiss He had given from above and somehow
that made me yearn even more deeply for Thee
wanting also to be caressed, to feel His love in me
opening Your word, the dialogue begins
i hear His voice, i know it's Him.
unmistaken, the psalm take hold
stories, testimonies, written long ago
and yet they're current, timeless they be
whispered, listened to – by me…
and the day begins

sunrise 302

i'd forgotten the loveliness of early dawn
the light blue halo that rests upon
the landscape as He makes His way
across the horizon at the beginning of the day
holy pure and sacred it be
silent, simple yet majestic is He
exhilarated once again am i
to see His presence in the sky.

sunrise 318

i hear a bird or two, their songs to sing
the merriment of being alive they bring
undeniable their refrain underlines
the truth of the breath i find
within my own chest and i can choose
to be thankful or too lose
the very things He wants me to hear
i'm not alone and He is here.

sunrise 702

"and then there was light" each mornings revisited
and so our quest… to be inquisitive
what lies ahead, what will the day bring
remembering to bow, first to my King
to honor the One who created the day
in thoughtful worship and simply say

"thanks be to God."

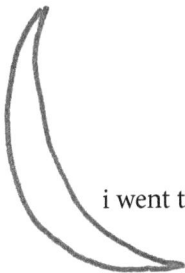

sunrise 279

i went to bed with an illuminated smile in the sky
the moonset was lovely as if Thy
hand had delivered, His salutation
from above, a warm and dear consolation
and then in the very earliest moments of dawn
once again my eyes rested upon
the smile, the imprint on which i'd fallen asleep
now still hung, so my memory would keep
His signature on my soul.

sunrise 321

a slight peach haze colored the dawn
like a mirror in a dressing room – it beautified the lawn
enhancing the morning, the blush of sunlight
so lovely His touch, how dear to my sight
i thank you Lord for your generous invocation
to day's beginning, a silent celebration
of Your presence and i glory in knowing
once again Your incarnation showing
dawn's early light.

9

sunrise 219

the trees silhouetted in dawn's early light
against a deep blue sky – such a delight
as the day begins – restore my anticipation
that once was alive, begin a restoration
within my being, replace this dread
and sorrow and sadness with Your joy instead
allowing the darkness of night to slip away
and letting the fullness of the light of day
renew.

sunrise 220

i'd forgotten how daybreak can truly fill
one's heart, one's mind, and one's will.
with Your intention, the joy of Your salvation
as resurrection illumination
fills the sky.

sunrise 221

fully opened, this letter He's designed
its capacity – an overflow into this world of mine
a bright sky is blue, a stillness that lay
upon the horizon of this brand new day.

sunrise 213

over and over and over, it does it again
a cup of tea, piping, soothing; my friend
bringing me to a place of comfort and peace
in the early morning hours, i find relief
a simple cup of tea, with milk and sugar
somehow the solutions to life's should've's
to sip or to gulp, to slowly take in
this measure of sweetness, wholly given by Him.

sunrise 218

just a hint of daylight beyond the tree line
a glimpse of hope from the Divine
i must not despair, His presence ever near
i need not worry, i need not fear
Your promise to me, You will never forsake
nor mankind has – to not mistake
Your love for the kind that disappears
light in the dark as You bring Yourself near.

sunrise 176

mornings rays so light, so new
presenting the day, a sky so blue
glints of lumina through the trees
bowed i am for on my knees
the sense of Your power and majesty
somehow becomes more real to me
dwarfed i am in humility
bent to worship my God and King.

sunrise 178

what am i believing this morning as i rise
with the sun streaming through the windowpane am i
questioning God through the circumstances i am living
rather than praising Him for what He is giving
can i allow myself to receive all this pain
as i did when i received gain
help me to remember Lord!

sunrise 47

a haze now to be as the sun settles in
the birds are singing once and again
glistening the trees, evidence of the storm
as if to sparkle, the leaves are adorned
a few drops from heaven, reminded am i
so many truths i'm told as i look to the sky
and beyond to the place of eternity
quietly He brings His words to me.

sunrise 53

i want to be patient, i want to be kind
i want to be loving, i want peace of mind
i want to be content, i want to be faithful
i want to be joyful, i want to be able
to live life fully and only in You
will i be enabled to do
all the above, Your Spirit in me.
so Lord before i even get out of bed let it be.

sunrise 43

another dark morning, rain continuously to fall
a shadow of misery brought such a pall
and i wonder will the whole day be
full of this reflection from inside of me
needful i am of your rescue, i ask
that this attitude of sorrow will not last
help me to rise above and see
the reason for Your sovereignty
though not understood, but accepted by me
and given i believe by the hand of Thee.

sunrise 45

so many mornings have been overcast
darkened the sky. how long will this last?
the oppression i feel, proclaimed in these days
hour after hour of rain – not gone away
perhaps in agreement, the heavens to weep
the sorrow of betrayal, promises not to keep
the mournful dove sings her song
nature's recognition that he is gone.

sunrise 370

the beginnings of distinguishment above the trees
a slight variation of color by Thee
ever so slowly the dawning of day
steady, methodical is His way
a pace unlike anything in the world
intentional grace to quietly unfurl
damask or silk or perhaps chiffon
the beauty of dawn, that He lays upon
the sky.

sunrise 430

a holy hallelujah, silence from above
the light of day. the warmth of His love
rains down in the early morning hours
a stilled repose – yet exposed His power
He's come to us, my God invites.
desiring we enter in to experience His light
will i negate His invitation
or with a holy resound – in celebration
accept and receive.

sunrise 340

peach tea or apple cider in the sky
the remains of sunrise, it's as if i
can drink in the refreshment He brings
the light of day – His silent ring!

"the trees of the Lord drink their fill..."
psalm 104:16a

sunrise 343

and ivory gold shown above the tree line
breakfast champagne, all glory divine
to raise a glass, a toast to our God
who has conquered and won the battle on this sod.
remembering the conquest and not the defeat
to drink in the flavor of morningtide sweet
whatever the day may present, to recall
the victory He won, to those who fall
at His feet.

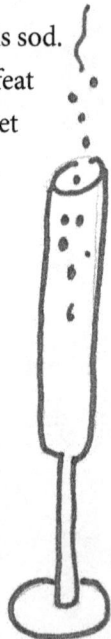

sunrise 369

up early enough to see the mystery
the pre-dawn colors the glide gently
across the heavens, in silent anticipation
of the Lord's sacred and sovereign navigation
morningtide.

sunrise 708

every morning the blinding sun
reminds me of stephen, the first martyred son
who smiled as he entered heaven's gate
this world to leave and not to forsake
can i too Lord be blinded today
oh perhaps in simple ways
that i may not be so attached
to what this world holds, the this and that
but instead to look above
reminded once again of His love
and step out in faith celebrating Thee
in all i do, and am and see. – amen.

sunrise 709

how sunlight awakens my soul
its beauty so easy, its majesty bold
without a sound it changes the landscape
of the earth and i cannot escape
what it does within my being
countless gifts that i am seeing
dancing across the window lace
changing the complexion of my face
growing the grass or browning a leaf
it is His presence that makes one meek –
Sonshine.

sunrise 726

the sky aglow inflamed it be
as i watch the power of Thee
a greeting high, His majesty
burning above for all to see
the orange, the purple, the magnitude
of glow and flame sweet gratitude
a mirror of the sacrificial altars from long ago
no longer needed, only His love aglow
good morning —

sunrise 801

the sunrise had quietly come and gone
no magnificent display of color this morning's dawn
instead a pale blue sky, ordinary time
and yet i heard Him say "be present, to this heart of Mine"
so to patiently wait with expectancy
the trail of ordinary and common to see
what the day will bring from Thee
to watch even more intently.

footprints

sunrise 805

today's dawning swept across the expanse
morningtide in a proverbial dance
a waltz of colors pink, purple and aqua marine
seen through the silhouette of autumn's falling leaves
what more could one ask for…
and now as heaven's music to fade
along with it the colors of dawn drifted away
what a privilege to sit and take the time to gaze
the splendor of His presence remembered
throughout the day.

"The people who were sitting in darkness saw
a Great Light, and
those who were sitting in the land and the
shadow of death,
Upon them a Light dawned."

matthew 4:16

sunrise 940

a cradle of light held in the barren limb
out of my window as morningtide to begin
the end of night, the moon's crescent
and just below it is dawn's essence
a blush color at the horizon line
a hue distinct and holy to define
the ebb of a new day on its way
as the cradle of the moon
slowly slipped away.

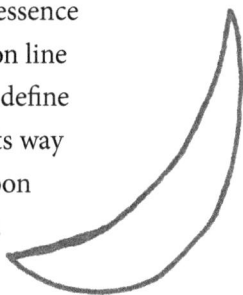

sunrise 941

so pale the blue, very light the sky
as a mother's touch for a baby's cry
feeling a tenderness within my being
my heart had been changed by what i was seeing
how oft that can happen if we allow
His breath in the deepest hollows –
of our souls

sunrise 946

"in Him was life and life was the Light of men."

john 1:4

can a daybreak sky actually be seen
without us being back into and onto Him
and a flash of lightning in a stormy sky
to hear Him say, it is I, it is I.
the beauty unmatched of sunsets glow,
His flame, His light wanting us to know
"in Him was life and life was the Light of men"
over and over with a silent amen –
He calls

sunrise 978

the morning sky even lighter it seems
for fallen snow reflects and gleams
a paradise of white, dazzling it be
the Son of God created it for me
and so i begin my day,
thinking of Him and His amazing ways
he chooses to delight those of us on earth
beautiful pleasures, He does birth
for us to see and to enjoy –
His magnificent grace to employ –

Hallelujah

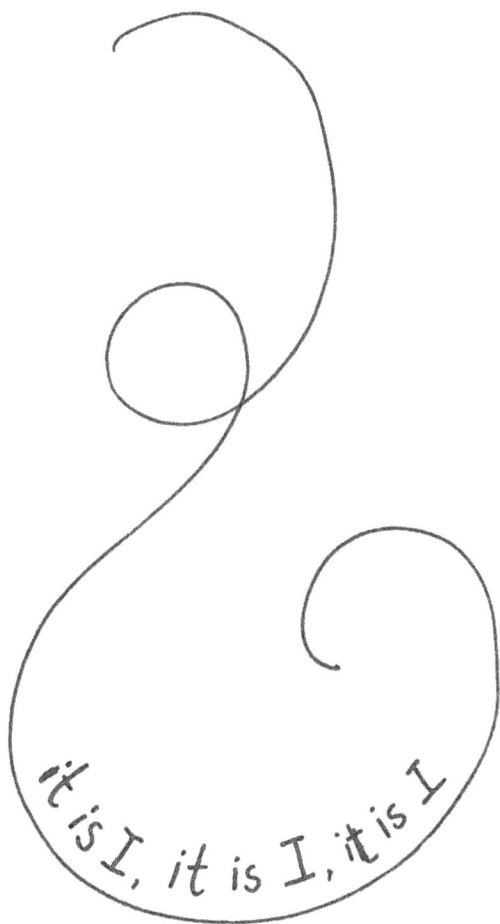

it is I, it is I, it is I

thoughts

i offer these meager thoughts –
to others for i believe i ought
for they have come directly by Thee
when in His company i to be
hearing His heart, upon my own
impression from the One on the throne
onto paper, recorded in time
that they be no longer mine,
but His sweet whispers brought to me
and shared, i hope that others may see –
Him

thoughts 115

all too soon to fade not even a hint
of color left in the sky, only a glint
of sunlight – yet all else has been erased
except perhaps upon each face –
like moses off of the mountain to shine
so the glow in each countenance to find
if one is willing to portray His company
held in our expressions for others to see.

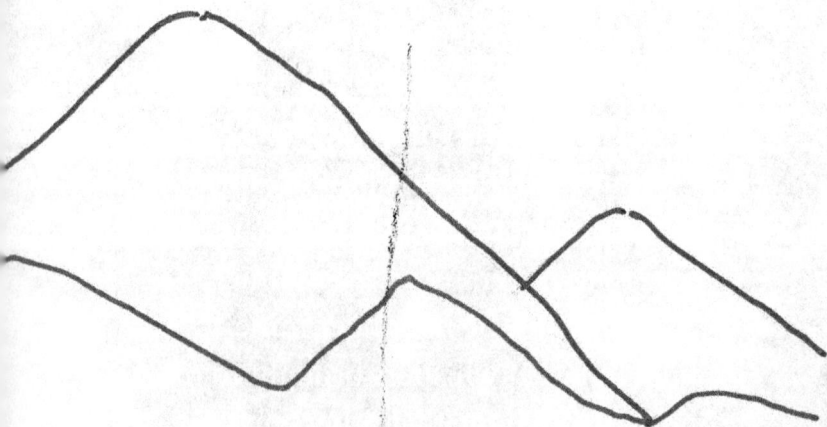

thoughts 121

i watch as the naked branches bare themselves
to the wind, the elements and i think to myself
am i willing to bare all of me
into the wind of His Spirit that i might be
exposed, stripped of anything undesired
the tugging and pulling that transpires
a branch from its spring and summer attire
to autumn's change and then winter's desire
help me Lord to be completely undone –
by Thee, my soul and heart won

thoughts 144

i sit and wait with a knowing anticipation
of sunrise, dawn, His glorious invitation
into the truth, each life to experience resurrection
portrayed by His inclusive presentation
though all will not receive the powerful illustration
mankind arrogant and full of hesitation
others will believe and begin the transformation
joining with all the saints in a holy celebration
thanks be to God!

thanks be to God

thoughts 180

i do remember when
the sky wasn't continually gray and then
i was able to feel the embrace of life
that was connected to being a wife
was it circumstances, i suppose so,
but in truth i didn't know...
for His love was also in my heart
the two didn't seem to be set apart,
but now, since my husband has left
a constant gray – for i'm bereft –
the human countenance reflects this life
it remains in pain and in strife
yet my heart continues to grow in Thee
i'm grateful, thankful, that it is He
who keeps me buoyed, though daily the loss
i remember His sacrifice upon the cross

thoughts 11

1,000 times at least or more
i've read, or seen or heard Him pour
His words spoken to my trembling heart
so very clear He to impart
whatever messages He wants to record
i simple transcribe these words from the Lord
only later to read and gain
a perspective that could've only been lain
by God above – for who but He
could have given the words to me

thoughts 302

frost is on the lawn not long to last
for the sun is overhead and its task
to melt the frost so it may water
the very land that lies under
each of us have been assigned
a task, an effort we're to find
often we think wherever we are
we must go someplace else – but just how far
are we to travel to determine
the works we're to accomplish, in earnest
perhaps it's easier than we conclude
not to be arrogant or to be thought of as rude,
but what if it's in the everyday
the routine of life that shows us the way
changing a diaper – a wee one to comfort
actions that have become habit,
but given to as for purpose to perform
deeds to mature draw others and form
lives into torches that they may all be
luminaries, to lead others to Thee…

silently

thoughts 304

holy water as a tear to shed
a movement of Your Spirit, holiness fed
a wonder we often want to avoid
or apologize and yet it's Him employed
oh Father help us to realize that Thee
is a presence within, eternally
filled we are Your essence to flow
a tear shed, You desire us to know it's You!

thoughts 18

how does Your love make a difference in my life?
to ponder over, thinking not once but twice…
am i able to love and sacrifice more
because of the love that you have poured
(romans 5:5)
into my heart,
am i able to discern
the needs of others and then to learn
how i can be about Your business, that they
will come to faith – not wait another day
do others see your love in me
is it an invitation to be…
held in the arms that were outstretched
upon the cross – You gave Your best –
how does Your love make a difference in one's life?

thoughts 395

later and later the sun to bed
longer the evenings, and it has been said
with hours more to celebrate the day
much foolishness can be displayed
will that be the case in my own life to live
so easy it is the impression to give
of righteousness yet mindful one must be
of the true thoughts and motives within me
cleansed by His word and at the confessional i find
it is the only way to rest and have peace of mind

thoughts 373

i watched as the bluish green
branches waved, orchestrated they seem
dancing to a current i could not feel or hear
for there was a closed window and
that lay between us, yet i wanted to kick up my heels
for they exhibited such appeal
a wellness to the response of His will,
but before the wind, how long had they been still?

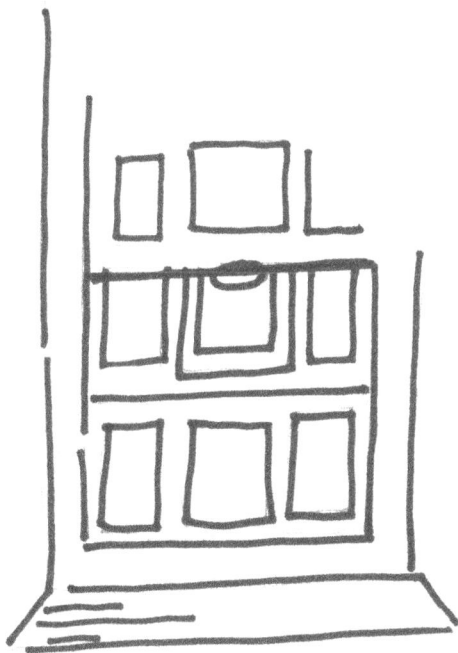

thoughts 349

"o Lord i love the habitation of Your home, and the place
where Your glory dwells – do not take my soul away
along with sinners nor my life with men of bloodshed
in whose hands is a wicked scheme and whose right hand
if full of bribes – but as for me i shall walk in my
integrity redeem me and be gracious to me. my foot
stands on level place in the congregations i shall
bless the Lord."

psalm 26:8-12

corruption is such a subtle movement in our soul
it's so interesting how it can grab ahold
without even a wince, for often to answer
the very thing that we are after
position, power, to just be recognized
thought of as special in someone's eyes
a slip here and there and soon to find
we've settled upon what was in our minds
but how did we get there what actions conceived
when did we start to go against what we believe
when our affections and desires became
more important than Your name

thoughts 20

invisible influence felt but not seen
a person who has died, but their presence has been
registered within the walls of our hearts
however long or short not to depart
and then to be carried in our thoughts and actions
a momentary life, just a fraction,
but forever changed by the breath they breathed
oh Lord thank You for Your truth received

rest in
peace

thoughts 46

how am i to be a city on a hill
light streaming out, His perfect will
generous, thankful, loving others where they be
no expectation; only anticipation in Thee
receiving in His love, blessing others with the same
all done for His glory and in His name
a lighthouse, a beacon drawing others to Him
glory Hallelujah – the "night" of earth is dimmed

*"surely goodness and loving kindness will follow me all the
days of my life and I will dwell in the house of the Lord forever,"*
psalm 23:6

*How great is Your goodness, Which You have stored up for
those who fear You. Which You have wrought for those who
take refuge in You. Before the sons of men!*
psalm 31:19

*But the fruit of the Spirit is love, joy, peace, patience, kindness,
goodness, faithfulness, gentleness, self control against such
things there is no law.*
galatians 5:22-23

*To this end also we pray for you always that our God will
count you worthy of your calling, and fulfill every desire for
goodness and the work of faith with power.*
II thessalonians1:11

thoughts 52

tonight my heart feels like an empty jewelry box
one that held treasures, the velvet lining mocks
holding impressions of what was kept
within its walls not able to forget
the ring we selected. flowers to line
this gold band, our hands intertwined
a circle of diamonds to sparkle and shine
remembering how taken love was fine
a silver heart formed into a ring
for 25 years of marriage and here's the thing
the empty treasure box tarnished by my tears
and wishing that he was still here

thoughts 71

Your Spirit dictates and i respond
it's an amazing gift to this vagabond
that needs not to understand,
but only take pen in hand
readied, willing to jot down
whatever words tumble to page and sound –
listening intently at the oddest times
often evoked by a queer sign
that may have meant nothing to another passing by,
but out You scroll to testify
to the most ordinary that now has become
extraordinary and i'm undone

thoughts 78

it came out in a conversation i was having
how does one receive gentleness, abounding…
allowing, letting, welcoming in
this nebulous idea that originates in Him
the tenderness of another to let that flow
into my being so i'll begin to know
perhaps even perceive it as a tangible thing
ah the reality of gentleness to begin
a gesture that beckons one to come closer
an intimacy of sincerity, not that of a jokester
like the color of blue in the morning sky
there, but just subtly spied…
able to change the heart at a glance
allowing anothers gentleness a chance
then the thought occurs to replicate
and ever so slowly we learn to navigate
the streams of gentleness, in part to abide
letting the Lord lead our stride.
a touch, a word, a thought in deed
gentleness has begun, this i believe

*"But the fruit of the Spirit is love, joy, peace, patience,
kindness, goodness, faithfulness, gentleness, self control.
against such things there is no law."*

galatians 5:22-23

thoughts 127

the rise had stained the sky momentarily so,
as if kissed, His lips pressed hard wanting us to know
He'd sealed the day whatever it to bring
the give and the take would be from Him –
utterly free to dance or to just linger about
to skip, to run, to sing and the shout
whatever content the day might hold
He was standing with me as it to unfold –

sealed with a kiss...

thoughts 97

my favorite penpal is Thee
whether in the sky to see
or felt in my spirit and then
to pen the occasion so when
i'm not sure of His mail to come
i remember His last postcard, some
awesome bird call to be heard
or the glistening lake though no words
used to transmit He continues to write
a yellow finch on winged flight
the aftermath of a sudden storm
and now a rainbow to be born
salutations from my God
the script of *God*

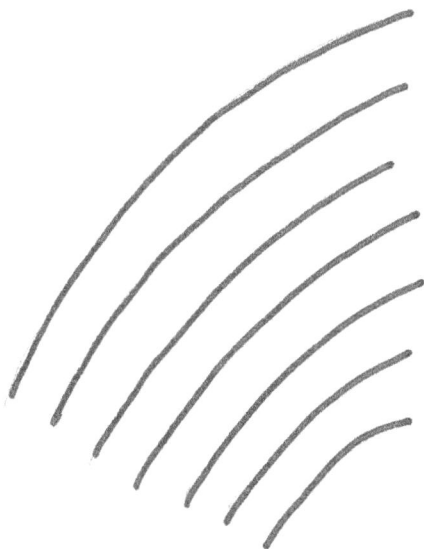

thoughts 115

the divine seamstress is He
each design altered as it was meant to be
tailor made we are from up above
each stitch placed through His infinite love
adjustments made, hemlines changed
His specifications to remain
as life is lived a loving creation
the wonder of His contemplations

thoughts 185

i wonder is an opinion always to become
a judgment of another when day is done
how is it possible to have our minds set on Thee
for only then can our true identity
be in His love – received and accepted
adoption by the Lord, yet by the world rejected
knowing within our hearts we are His child
and not by others' opinions compiled
when will we learn to listen to the Spirit's voice
in prayer and contemplation may i be led to that choice –

amen –

*"But as many as received Him, to them He gave the
right to become children of God, even to those who
believe in His name."*

john:12

thoughts 273

the gift of His presence in a cup of tea
or looking out upon the sky blue sea
praying as each letter i pen
wherever it to arrive, wherever it i send

to have a bit of the Spirit's grace
His presence endowed upon its space
words spoken to one who arrives
greeted with His kindness, a welcoming prize

His presence to go forth from me
a windfall of mercy to be
delivered because i have spent
time with my God and He has lent –
His love

thoughts 43

the austramaria, as if the flower trumpets could sound
vibrant cranberry and yellow throats how would they
sound?
i wonder in heaven will they be given a
voice
And what else that's now silent will be given a
choice
to shout the praises of our King
will anything be silent without a song to sing?
and will the praise be constant and throughout
not a reaction, but rather a mighty shout.

thoughts 500

the grass has greened as i look out to see
morning's light, how beautiful it be
it seems as though the calendar days
are swiftly passing by, time has a way
of slipping through our fingers and our minds
without purpose so easy to find
a blur instead of meaningful time
being wholly present and able to find
changing a diaper, or cleaning the table
simple tasks, but pleasure is able
to be found when accomplished they be
through the strength and grace for Thee

nature

His nature is our nature too
the earth its beauty to care for and view
seldom do our thoughts coincide
though His desire is for us to abide
watch and see the wonder displayed
and all the hope He has made.

nature 242

i always think i've already seen
the most beautiful sunset that's ever been
and then i'm drawn to the window and lo and behold
the glory of His artistry in blue and gold
is so lovely that aloud i declare
maybe today is the one and to be fair –
how many times i've said this i really don't know,
but i realize He uses it to grow
me up in anticipation of what He to bring
mindful i am of His imaginings –

nature 66

angels' harps or a gentle whistling wind
perhaps if i stop and listen again
i'll be able to distinguish which it be
or maybe i'll let my imagination see
what i want and so the angels play
a sweet, sweet song amongst the trees to lay
and silently the forest and vale now rest
upon a sparkling and white breast
of snow

nature 7

purple blue wonder had now invaded
the heavens above, as if a faded
vellum was set high in the sky
awaiting His hands, a message to spy –
the trees still barren in their winter attire
bordered His stationery, and then a fire
in the distance a glint of scarlet to rise
and soon the vellum transfigured before my eyes
only He could transcribe a message this way
in brilliant color – so eloquent to say –
i love you, remember as you go through your day
allowing yourself not to forget what I say

nature 516

unidentifiable their songs so sweet
first one then another drowning out the defeat
that seems to want to rear its ugly head –
yet song is stronger instead of dread.

*"But about midnight Paul and Silas were praying and singing
hymns of praise to God, and the prisoners were listening to
them..."*

acts 16:25

destroyed was the victory of the enemy that day
so within my heart i choose also to lift
my voice in collaboration – His triumph to shift
whatever the enemy might have in mind –
to the desire of my God – the tranquility and
peace of mind

nature 564

blossoms of so many colors displayed
scarlet, yellow, white and the rain played –
with the pear tree and the tulip and daffodil
spreading their petals, the earth is thrilled
with this season of folly and fragrance to dance
embraced, we are – His love enhanced
by all that nature has to share
the beauty, the essence of springtime fare

nature 591

from flower, to sprout, then leaves to be
fully engaged in it's purpose, the tree
the clouds to form, to fill and then pour
their contents, the rain, watering the earth's floor
it rises, brings light and warmth as it shines
then darkens the day for rest us to find
hyacinth stocks in paradise colors
purple, pink and white, their fragrance like
none other
in green pastures each blade of grass
a bed of comfort in psalm 23 to last…
each of these their design to become
drawing agents for His Kingdom
and so the question then begs to be asked
how about each of us – have our lives met
the task
that we've been created for and by Thee
in a unique way, you and me?

*"The Lord will accomplish what concerns me; Your loving
kindness, O Lord is everlasting. Do not forsake the works of
Your hands."*

psalm 138:8

nature 595

i see the branches sway in the wind
free to accept the breeze from Him
i see the color of the sky so blue
and in my heart no wonder, as to where the
command or from who
i see a daffodil, from bulb to trumpet be
heed the wish, that comes from Thee
i see the stain of violet as the sun to rise
an echo of the Lord's presence on high
i see an infant fresh from the womb
given life and breath and oh so soon
to choose a willfulness that nature does not concede
and only time will tell if the wee one to believe

nature 596

a beautiful violet caught in the springtime boughs
so lovely as whips of color bend and bow
with the wind, on this late april day
the world so full of color, as the Lord has His way
how would each of our lives differ if we
allowed Him full reign, perhaps to be
as the wind in the trees, lovely to bend
in worship and praise of our Lord, amen!

nature 684

the wind in the trees the color of a bird's wing
these may be some of the most important things
in ones day to simply not dismiss,
but give them room and hopefully not miss
a word, or conversation He desires with me
it's in the silence or the quiet of Thee
that can draw us if we allow our hearts to hear
the message He presents to these who have an ear

nature 58

a correspondence ordered by God
as i experience creation, on this earthly sod
relating to a breeze my dance partner it be
or the thunder that warns like a friend is he
fragrance, her perfume in which i stand
simply taking in the pleasure, given to man
the sound of rain and the silence of snow
He's written to us and wants us to know
He's with us. God's correspondence

nature 73

to hear the sounds of nature, to let them in
i must open my back door or the din
of traffic and mankind's bustle takes over
instead of the wind and the fragrance of clover
and when i allow myself the time to absorb
there truly is so much more
that would have been overlooked
had i not tarried

nature 76

their skirts, the wind, had caught their leaves
twirled and twisted, dancing with ease
to watch, to gaze their swirling and then
an easy dropping of leaves to descend
a jig, a sway, this way and that
i watched with wonder now as the trees sat
motionless, awaiting their partner's arrival
to move them again as part of their survival

nature 77

the pine, the aspen, the birch and blue spruce
all, so i looked out at all, the abundant earth
shrubs and flowers, fauna galore
purple and green, pink and yellow so much more
than i to record, rather to just be immersed
in God's kindness, to simply rehearse
the acceptance of His abundant grace
and to wear its expression upon my face –

nature 716

often i hear people speak of the mountains or the ocean
that to visit those places is the quotient
the arena in which they can finally hear
His voice speaking to them loud and clear,
but i believe we need not fireworks displayed
to hear exactly what He has to say
its often in the whisper of the wind
or the fragrance of fleshly mowed grass that sends
a dialogue from Him to me –
for i believe that silence is the key
an inward peace that then pervades
the place i am on any given day
and the explosion of energy to take place
happens within and throughout by His grace
the electricity of walking with Him i find
a power only described as divine

nature 720

it looked as if the wild wheat had gone to war
with the rain in the last week, for it was no more
the deluge had destroyed what grew alongside the road
no need to attend the tall grass or mow
for the storms had bent and bowed each stalk
a battlefield…if you can imagine that –
laid to rest…so to speak
survival of the fittest, not the meek.

nature 721

oh the landscape as if i could taste
the seamline of the horizon, the beauty to baste
my much needed soul with His exquisite hand
No longer parched i became as the sky and land
rose up before me – there's something about
where they meet –
its as if a bit of heaven to greet
for the artistry uncomparable it be
the hemline of God's mystery

nature 728

how sweet the sound of morningtide
upon the earth, before one's stride…
the curtains dance as a springtime breeze
blows through the screens with such ease
and the robin's who lead the chorale today
singing and serenading, start the parade
my dwelling place is with Thee and i
am thankful so thankful for the rise.

nature 744

the monarch and the mulberry
were enjoying the light
sunshine from above gave hope and delight
to each living creature, or fauna and i
got to watch as they smiled and winked
at the sky

nature 748

the grass held droplets of mornings dew
His signature across the landscape to insure
each wonder that He's created, this season of spring
come to the fountain, living water He brings
to not only the grass... and the evergreen trees
that have been delighted with the rain and remember
Thee
by being so proud, their boughs displayed
a blue spruce pine captures my view and i say
wow!

nature 749

sunlight streams through every windowpane
His glory shone – to call His name
to be amazed at each detail He provides
i think He to whisper to confide
in each of us not an hour to go by
where in His soft stillness not to testify
to His great love and the yearning for our hearts
in most unusual ways He does impart

*His hesed**

nature 752

the beauty of another day born
warm spring air, as if a page torn
from the book of eternity for perfect it be
the sounds, the sights, to be with Thee
the songs that were being sung were so very sweet
they lightened my heart and the steps to my feet
above all the noise that mankind can make
the sounds of nature were to celebrate
thanks be to God!

*Hesed indicates faithfulness to a relationship

nature 766

self sacrifice, like a flower to the sun
opened to the warmth and dying has begun
more to be shared and the closer we become
to deaths door, the journey to the Son
letting our lives spent for each other
enriched we are by one and another
sharing the dance, letting our love to be
given away most graciously
by His Spirit

nature 794

the birds now their songs to be heard
rain has passed, the storm deferred
farther east the words to carry
the deluge upon the earth to make merry
that which needs the moisture to grow
in His infinite wisdom He to know
and the melodies that now reign
is a pleasure in which cannot be contained

"Sing to God, O kingdoms of the earth,
Sing praises to the Lord."
selah

psalm 68:32

nature 803

the earth has been treated to an abundant drink
storms over night and the rain to sink
deep into the soil, and the posture i suppose
of all the flowers tells me so
day lilies shining a pure gold
many of the rose buds to now unfold
potted plants so many varieties to name
His touch to behold and they to claim
His glory

nature 807

the dew lay thick on the porch floor
covering the deck chairs and so much more
a glistening to each leaf and branch
God's inventive way to simply enhance
the beauty seen – through the early morning light
to take in this concert of pure delight
grateful so very grateful for His gift given
from Thee to me – presented, the gloves of heaven

nature 812

the breath of the Spirit bowed the tall grass
so simple and beautiful, as if romanced
a dance that i was able to observe and take in
it was as if swing dancing was created by Him
bowed, to swirl and then once again erect
the wind; the tall grasses partner to direct
sychronized, yet as though unplanned
the great difference between God and man

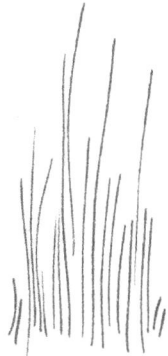

nature 859

each morningtide a victory heralded
often silent – the colors, the contrast –
no mistakes or errors –
rather His mastery often displayed
in the sun, the clouds, His autograph
His name –
can one be grateful for each breath taken
a new day to be celebrated – for we not forsaken,
but rather like baby chicks gathered in His arms
awakened, reminded, in His love –
there's no harm –

nature 867

from a brilliant blue and a gleaming white
to a dusty gray and filtered light
i ask myself if i had missed the rise
the days portrayed would otherwise
have been what now has settled in
instead of the glory presented by Him

nature 119

holiness as seen in a leaf's vein
in a single snowflake, or a drop of rain
the softness of a newborn's skin
gathered around a Christmas tree
again and again
set aside – these events in time
spawn worship of the divine
life's wonder ordinary or not they be
they do remind us that it is He
we are to worship

nature 155

it's somewhat easier i think it be
to revere God when a glorious sunset i see
or spring's first robin when on a budded branch
to perch
and when finding a lost treasure after a mighty search
than it is when a casket to close
or the diagnosis that you suspected and now know
of the emotion that be before me
yet God hasn't changed…

nature 191

to be held in one's mind, like a flower freshly picked
nature – the colors, the wonder, a mood to be switched
from utter loneliness and despair
to praise and hallelujahs, steeped in His care,
but one must take the time to simply be
no hurry, no rush, but rather in Thee
i find my home, complete, no need to stray
instead to be, to imagine and play

nature 204

i was awakened by the footprints of falling rain
as they danced and paraded across the roof and
windowpanes
two or three times they kicked up their heels
as if a celebration, a joyous appeal
and i was drawn in, included was i
was part of the party though not to spy
for i resisted wanting to stay reclined
a bit more rest i needed to find

nature 388

a peach drenched dawning sky
its beauty i drink in for i
am thirsty for His presence within
confessing all known and unknown sin
oh Father, anger has risen inside
the past is present and i can't abide
forgiveness again needs to reign
within my heart may you sustain
the parts of me that are of You
and wholly change my attitude
more than a prayer, a plea to Thee
Father God change all of me

*"Let them give thanks to the Lord for His lovingkindness,
And for His wonders to the sons of men! For He has
satisfied the thirsty soul. And the hungry soul He has
filled with what is good."*

psalm 107:8 8-9

nature 384

butterflies to flutter, flowers on wing
filling the garden, a holy offering
as if Your laughter and mirth from above
has come into our lives – evidence of Your love
oh, Holy One of Israel, how you attest
of Your grace-giving, Your sacred best
help me to remember and allow me to be
everything You desire-the wonder of Thee

colors

colors that are yet to be named
created by our God, His fame
incredible, yet He hints in the still
and draws us in to see His will
a favorite shade or tint He prepares
at sunrise or maybe noon time fare
blazing or subdued they be
all to declare the attributes of Thee

color 56

breathtakingly beautiful the blue shadows cast
on the snow upon the earth, winter's blast
that covered the lawns and changed the landscape
lovely so lovely – one cannot escape
the beauty portrayed, how wonderful the sound
the crunch of snow under foot, upon the ground
to celebrate the season, to enjoy what's bestowed
rather than, to complain about the snow.

color 59

the many shades of sapphire seem to be present in the sky
a tidal wave of glory – as with His hand He passes by
light on the horizon and to fill the atmosphere
stunning subtlety for the Lord is here
awakened to His presence through it or His word
yet silent, oh, so quiet – never a sound to be heard
a holy salutation, impressed upon my being
whether through my vision or what i am reading
He is here.

color 57

the color of the sky was sparkling blue
deep and rich and stunning the shade, the hue
how much delight i garner from high above
the beauty is beyond words – simply His love
come down

color 51

oh, purple cast of december air
it is Thine advent a holy fare
that rises and covers the days beginning
so sacred is the silent inning
and then Your daybreak evolves and i
get to observe, as if to spy
from within the comfort of my abode
void of the wind and the cold

color 64

streaks of tangerine and turquoise too
out my kitchen window a spectacular view
Your kindness spread like orange marmalade
as it oozes and expands 'til fully laid
across the heavens – all glory given
to God on high for holy wrappings and ribbons
that fill the atmosphere and we here below
can only ooh and ah at what You've bestowed

color 265

a golden orange was all we were seeing
the beauty foretold – if one was believing
in the future that awaits for us in eternity
the blazing of the sun captured that truth to see –
perspective where does it come from and where does it lead
wherever we start from, it to seed
the rest of our thoughts, so the bible to read
then our perspective the truth on which to feed

color 269

the palest of sherbet was dished up for one to delight
as if to taste, as if to take a bite
of eventides arrival, the end of another day
in sweetness and quietude; God's way –
i find myself in wonder of His thoughts
defining His character, He has brought
me to a place of solitude and peace
stilling my mind and finding release
through His canvas of grandeur

color 282

peacock feathers surely what was on His mind
as the sun rose and the colors of the sky to find
were a duplicate of what i had seen
peacock feathers high above was the scene
inventive, unpredictable, yet glorious too
the wonder displayed the indescribable to view

color 301

caught up in the branches, scattered wisps
of fuchsia and pink, to make one think
are these scraps from His cutting table
dropped upon the rise – if only we were able
to see beyond, but perhaps only to imagine
the work of His hands – only to fathom

color 531

the hyacinths lined the church walk
a vibrant, purple blue, was each stalk
pungent the fragrance so lovely it be
on the path, to the church to lead
it made me think of how heaven might
be similar in nature and oh what a sight
i conjured up, for a brief moment and i
was lifted to my imagined paradise
in the sky —

color 318

sunrise surprise, much earlier now
the days bloom, the light His power
switched upon the horizon, azure the sky
a pale topaz jeweled and i am breathless

color 327

black, purple, blue to fade
a bit of crimson to slip far away
an ivory white slate, my sins forgiven
through the horror of His torture we've been given
new life, a new day, to begin anew
to be told of salvation, as morningtide to view

color 509

the landscape had thirsted and answered it be
continual rain to drink deeply
and the effects were spread far and wide
colors to appear before our very eyes
spring green and the striking pigment of daffodils
trees to bud and the anticipation and thrill
of the array of color and fragrances to come
oh, just a foretaste of His kingdom

color 251

the sea of blue that lies overhead
was ever so lovely, perhaps He shed
a robe of sapphire as he to intercede
at the throne of God, and we believe
we can ask, in prayer for what we desire
He hears our voices and the Spirit's fire
consumes each request and then to be
translated into the will of Thee

"every single grace comes to the soul through prayer"
— st faustina

color 535

violet strands weaved into morningtides shade
as it slowly appears and silently parades
across the horizon, so bold and enlightening
there is nothing more that is so exciting
then the opening of each and every day
enlivened i am, for it takes my breath away
thanks, be to God!

color 539

streaks of indigo and deep deep blue
mix with sapphire and other hues
as morningtide splashes unto the shore
the beauty is more than hoped for
nature has stilled to watch in awe
as He commands the lovely dawn
delight brought to our bedside
awake dear one as He confides
in us

"Deep calls to deep at the sound of
Your waterfalls; all Your breakers
and Your waves have rolled over
me. The Lord will command His
lovingkindness in the daytime..."

psalm 42:7, 8

color 13

the fields were green, as far as one could see
mid-summer and the rains had appropriately
fallen to give the land and crops all they needed
to thrive, so that a harvest would succeed
thank God for His abundance that i'm able to view
across the nebraska landscape issued –
to pause and allow His grace to fill
my heart with hallelujahs, what a thrill!

color 64

the rise had colored the sky a splendid melon
as if a treat to digest, much sweeter than a lemon
how can a color bring such comfort to one's soul
ahh it be His hand in nature to behold –
and when the revelation comes to our being
such a mystery, and wonder is included in what we're seeing

color 35

and the sky a place to lay my head
1,000 stars my pillowcase, a galaxy wed
as vast as an ocean, as blue as a sea
oh the wonder, and the comfort of Thee
my Bridegroom His universe displayed
and He my thoughts to invade
"go to sleep dear one, rest in Me
starship wonder – forever in My embrace are thee"

color 89

a light pewter, the distant palette
it brings a silent peace after
worrisome thoughts wanted to crowd
my heart, my head and yet somehow
Your canvas into which i stare
has brought me to remembering Your care
and i am comforted by Your desire to reach
wherever we are and to provide peace

color 726

the underbellies of the distance clouds
outlined in pearl dust somehow...
each blade of grass so very green
picture perfect – like a magazine
the evergreens, and pines hold such a luster
and the flower bouquets each and every cluster
are more beautiful than one can imagine
His hand upon the earth, and we to fathom
what paradise will one day be –
back to the garden of eternity

color 746

daisies that stood tall, as high as my waist
lavender and roses – just to give you a taste
of the garden i was enjoying as a breeze blew
the perfumed air and the sky so blue
such exquisite colors and fragrances He
designs
i do believe only could they be conceived
in God's mind
and we in our arrogance think that we –
can top any wonder from the likes of Thee

color 834

glorious, beautiful the sunrise delight
orange and pink and gleaming white
the clouds were dancing, an actual parade
so stunning this morningtide, to You we pray
let this be an omen of all that will take place
a holy inspiration of Your caring and Your grace
such wonder and majesty, take in to hold
as the beauty of daybreak continues to unfold

color 121

all but forgotten the colors of autumn gone
an early snowfall to rest upon
the sod, now covered over any hint
of orange, or cranberry not even a glimpse...
but wait a single leaf to lay
upon the snow mounds, it got away
and so i admire its spunk for it be
as if a mini flame on this cold, cold sea

color 125

the morning sky was aflame
each cloud outlined with a crimson stain
His glory blinded anyone who looked
directly into the sun and literally took
their eyesight away at least momentarily
the beauty was over the entire territory
such delight to let the day begin
to celebrate once and again…

with Thee

color 192

the sky a huge pastel of radiant pink
for above the color i see to think
a massive celebration taking place
and our sky just a reflection of the wonder
embraced.
to imagine a carol of bells
ringing forth in jubilation to tell
of joy and resounding glee, but we see
only the beauty of the pastels in the heavenlies

color 161

that most unusual color of sunrise appeared again
lovely to watch, to see it ascend
in the morningtide sky an audience of one
to make note of its beauty, this day has begun…
and so if the sun has dressed this day
in amazing apparel, in a stunning way
how can i join the theme
colossians 3:12-17 comes to mind in my remembering
putting on a heart of compassion to gently bear
with one another, His kindness to share
and may the peace of Christ rule in my heart
His word to richly dwell within – as i make a new
start —

color 283

layers of blue upon the dawning sky
so beautiful, only to stare if i
am so very grateful to the Lord who displays
His imagination throughout the day

high above or in a field far and wide
on a mountain top or by my side
filling me with wonder, drawn again and again
into His presence, my Saviour and friend

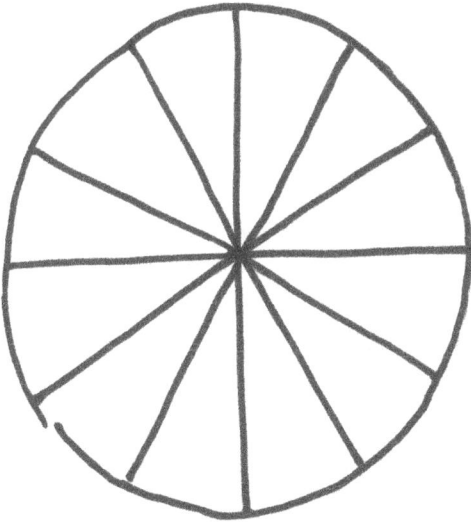

God's colorwheel

seasons

seasons are the color wheel
my God His artistry holds such zeal
to only stop and be enlightened by these
sent i believe to witness and please
His great power in the blazing harvest field
or the tenderness of a crocus bud and its appeal
silent snowfall or a summer breeze
delight yourself in all of these

the seasons teach us lessons in waiting
each year begins winter's white aiding
to the moisture that the soil desires
and through the silence and the calendar miles
the earth is readied and spring begins
to find its way home again –
a crocus or two, the bulbs to no longer wait
more sunshine and through the dirt they break
the snow to melt at its own pace
and soon to make room for the grace
of summer, when the temperatures rise
such fragrances in the air, yet always a surprise
and then the colors of the trees to change
from green, to orange and red to remain
until strong winds that autumn brings
all these seasons, all these happenings
are decided upon by the watchcare of God
not mankind upon this sod –
and we to watch in anticipation
a silent attentiveness – and a lesson in waiting

seasons 787

sparkling frost upon the ground
as if sprinkled and spread around
much like manna and so i wonder
is it to recall – the miracles under
the ordinary of this life to see
in parables did He not speak of these
things on which our eyes to fall
were put there perhaps to recall
Thee

seasons 207

twisted boughs, naked, then foliage stripped
a leaf here or there, but otherwise gripped
by the dress that only winter provides
darkened bark and awaiting the temps that abide.
stalwart and strong, building strength to withhold
the weather that is a part of the season to behold
do we also prepare and ready ourselves
for the season ahead –

seasons 332

looked out my window and as if to appear
the scriptures to come alive, truly brought near
for the temperature unseasonably high for this, time of year,
but upon the grass, as though manna brought near
i looked and blinked and looked once again
for i had just read the manuscript when
He had given them manna like snow it lay
and i was speechless, no words to say –
of course it was frost though high in the sky
the sun was ablaze, tears in my eyes –
He wanted me to believe just a glimpse of their story
to revisit with a touch of reality, history's glory
and i did.

seasons 352

hydrangea blossoms, daffodil trumpets, and rose petals
the gifts of nature, that steeled my metal
they continue though we'd gotten inches of snow
the flowers inside, helped me to know
that soon would come the evidence of spring
the end of february and soon to bring
daylighte savings time, buds on the trees
birdsongs to awaken me, these favorite things
would soon return, more breath to my step
winters concession soon to be met

seasons 443

the grass has turned from brown to green
and clouds up above, what will they bring?
perhaps spring time showers, they say we need rain
if that's true, then He the land to sustain
to just observe the seasonal changes
He dresses each one, and rearranges
with such stealth – in amazement and wonder
this God we serve, we His footstool under

seasons 300

the feathered finery of the nearly sprung trees
against the backdrop of morningtide to please
only silhouettes, such beauty and awe
sent from our Creator for each to pause
and give thanks

seasons 324

oh the sweet tenderness of springtime fare
the birds their songs, meet us where
our hearts need to be touched in such a way
that a song from a tree limb lightens the day
He knows us so well, for He created
my inward soul, my essence has been invaded
by allowing earth's nature to bring a balm
so soothing to a busy mom —

i'm struck by all the beauty that's around
the color of the sky and the life in the ground
yesterday, i saw these marvelously striped
purple and white
crocus with bright yellow tongues so bright
and daffodils too, their trumpets to sound
though silent they were reverberation
in the ground –
spring had literally sprung and i a witness to
the fascination of His gifts – i'm a bit unglued!

seasons 624

the grass was glistening from last nights rain
and the birds were singing their glorious refrain
above the sky was just settling in
to the kind of blue that brings thoughts of Him
for who but our Creator could set each day
to be an unexpected wonder, the glories of may –
thank You, o Lord, for You do not tire,
but are steadfast no matter what transpires

seasons 625

my tree in the backyard has finally slipped
into it's summer attire, from blossom to tipped
each leaf in solid green – to wave in the breeze
the boughs and branches filled and move with ease
and more as i begin to notice the change
days and days of dark clouds and rain
have brought a vitality to the scenery
oh so much greenery –

thank You Lord!

"Awake, my glory!
Awake, harp and lyre!
i will awaken the dawn."

psalm 57:8

seasons 768

"You have made summer and winter"

psalm 74:17b

the holiness of spring was almost at the end
from sprigs and buds to blossoms that send
the fragrance of heaven right into our lungs
breathe in deeply for He's just begun
to treat us to the delights yet to come
for next is summer and the glory of His Sun
to warm the earth and our activities
swimming, enjoying a good read leisurely
appreciating the sanctification that He provides
through the seasons of the year can help us to thrive –
putting our lives in the Spirits palms
an oft missed exercise expressed in the psalm.

seasons 626

spring time breeze and glistening dew
the wonder of may everywhere to view –
greening limbs and grass to grow
telling us, letting us know
just how much He loves us so

seasons 830

the last day of spring so lovely it be
a slight breeze and the birds in the trees
are carrying melodies upon the wind
the Lord my God has won my heart once again
how can one not bow and be glad
for the joy of the Lord and the beauty of the land
an invitation offered each morningtide
to envelope ourselves with the gift of His stride

amen

seasons 647

the birds now are wildly singing
back and forth from one tree to another winging
so bright the morning so vibrant their songs
engaged and inviting the human throng
to join the parade, the worshiping celebration
allowing our hearts the exhilaration
that comes from the inside out
the Spirit to lead – a holy fount

seasons 28

a summer carol heard out my back door
heralding the sun light and the day as it pours
itself out. nature beckoning each human being
awaken dear ones – to all you can be seeing
dawning delight, a new day ahead
shake off the night, climb out of bed
arise to the splendor that He has commanded
be present and aware for the Lord has planned it.

seasons 7

the zinnias had actually doubled in bloom
exquisite the planters, the lawns as if loomed –
lavish the landscape, beauty everywhere
july 4th – the holiday; a picnic fare
one day at a time, healing paced
care and concern, friends that have graced
my days with their presence and also their prayers
thankful i am that He meet us there
at our point of need.

seasons 11

the fullness of a summer day
remarkable-an aroma that stays
on your clothing, clean and fragrant it be
as if the sun to impress it permanently –
such simple gifts He chooses to employ
drawing us close – for us to enjoy
receiving in His love freely given
the wall between earth and heaven
invisible —

seasons 14

a gardenia blossom; God's extravagant scent
how clever He be – His love that's meant
to perfume our lives, yet do we take the time
to smell the roses and enjoy the wine?
of life given to us – from His overflowing love
generous, gracious, always to impart
a treasure or two may i take in
each one that is given by Him —

seasons 35

no matter where one looks upon this season
Your dwelling places give us reason
to rejoice and praise Thee the God above
for His wondrous and unending love
the blossoms and blooms so lavish they be
colossal Your blessings all over me
let not a moment go by
that i not testify

to Your grace

seasons 208

only days away from autumn's start
my favorite season, a song in my heart
the temperatures have cooled to be
sweater weather, a relief in me

seasons 212

how can i paint in words to draw
the seasons contrast from summer to the raw
days of autumn weather that arrives
hidden in the tall grass pumpkins to thrive
orange poke-a-dots upon the landscape
God's sense of humor one cannot escape

seasons 138

it seems as if crickets have replaced
the songs of birds…as if erased
i hope not permanently, only with the rain
for if it be then the season has changed
and it's not time, too early to be
perhaps "signs" of autumn understandably,
but not to arrive and stay for then
the year is almost at its end

seasons 621

the brilliant and lush carpeting of autumn was at hand
dispersed by the october winds it was His plan
the orange and russet colors of fall to cover
reds and golden leaves i could hear myself utter
such wonder to parade across the landscape
captivated i was and i could not escape
the AWE – He had provided on this day
oh such joy in my soul to stay

*"...And in Your book were all written The days that were
ordained for me, When as yet there was not one of them."*
psalm139:16

seasons 627

i look and all the roadside fauna
has turned, the rich colors of the seasons glory
burnt sienna, golden strands
a holy paint brush guides His hands
immersed i am in the presenting treasures
that He bestows as if there's any
reason except His love showered down
from sunrise glory and to the ground

so many leaves have lost their lives
it is their supreme sacrifice
upon each bough they spryly appear
announcing that springtime is here
to grow and bud, and in the breeze
catching the wind, with such ease
summer shading they provide
each bough and limb open wide
and then the change – for stained they be
with autumn fun and fantasy
red, orange, yellow, whatever He to choose
ever so slowly their grip to lose
a momentary carpet perhaps to find
but then again the winds to mind
swept away now only a memory
very much the life in me

seasons 645

a leaf once green now deepest red
a face once young now infirmed in bed
the hours in a day to be counted out
from dawn the sun to rise and then lights out
years beginning- the season of winter to start
fall, the ending – the year to mark
beginnings ordained and also endings by Thee
our days are indeed measured by He

seasons 656

autumn reign was falling at a steady pace
burnt sienna, cranberry, as if a race
was taking place just beyond the window glass
soon the boughs fullness would not last
it was so beautiful to see this continual rain
laid upon the earth, the landscape now changed
to be able to simply enjoy and take in
delighted by the touch of Him

seasons 372

the horizon draped in flaming peach
expanding across the sky to reach
heavenward, God expressing Himself
an acclamation to everyone else
the day's been birthed, celebrate the 'tide
of morning song and all that's alive
praise His name, declare that He alone is worthy –
the Godhead Three

seasons 437

thunder and lightning beyond the curtains drawn
more storms tonight before the dawn
turned off the sprinklers, no need to water
God's my gardener – and so i ponder
what else He may be up to tonight
a lone star though distant bright
the aroma of autumn now in the air
late september, such comforting fare

seasons 443

ever present Your seasonal rhythm and change
in the landscape as You rearrange
the colors of the rise and the set
and also the trees as they flush and get
full of reds, orange, yellow and even brown
as their leaves slowly fall to the ground
unless of course the autumnal rains
cause there to be a carpet gained
and the limbs in a rush barren they be
holding out their boughs in worship of Thee
an example for us to replicate
naked before Thee to celebrate

His love

seasons 622

the leaves had turned on the lone tree
red and deep cranberry in the autumn breeze
beginning, they were now to cover the lawn
i wanted to appreciate them before they were gone
His breath it seems is stronger today
the season in full swing, i'd have to say-
how lovely the colors as if ablaze
on fire, but not consumed – hallelujah
today!

seasons 678

heaven's confetti held in the limbs of the trees
at just the right season, released with ease
september, october, by november almost done
the ground carpeted, the Lord's fun
His imagination seems to stretch –
our finite minds – for He holds the best
when will we rest in His care
the wonder of God and His magnificent flare!

seasons 734

the frost is on the pumpkin or so they say
and on the land, the porch, everywhere it lay
cold so cold, the morning it be
still autumn, but it feels like winter to me
bundled up in bed, covers to my chin
not wanting to budge to start again
what will this day hold – gray and mundane
only in Your word am i able to gain
perspective —

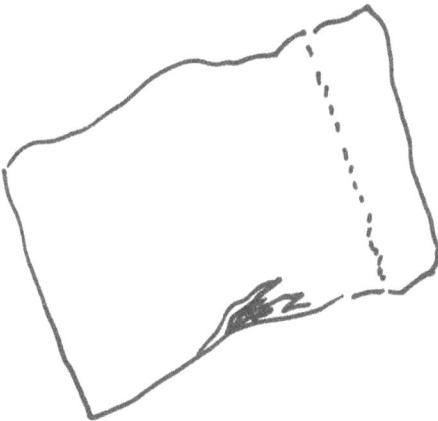

there really are no words for how He attends
to all of us here on earth, again and again
seasons that literally take my breath away
answers to unspoken prayers day after day
peace that remains no matter the circumstances
the joy i find in His word – not happenstance
thanksgiving fills my heart; november's theme
gratefulness to God for all that has been
and all that is to come with great anticipation
singing praises to the Lord with exhilaration!

seasons 12

each season as if a bottle of perfume and we
are somewhat aware if we choose to be
so much passes by, fragrance can seem
somewhat invisible, if you know what i mean
yet distinct for summer, winter, spring or fall
the burning leaves and we immediately
recall
a bonfire set and the autumn wind
carries the reminder to us again
or winters chill and the smell of evergreen
hot chocolate and woolen socks to bring
memories of springtime blooms so fresh and clean
summer once again – fresh green beans –
ah, the wonder

scripture

scripture

His word the tome on which i rely
the bible, His truth to testify
corrective, yet always lovingly
His rod and staff they comfort me
and help me not to wander too far away,
but with scripture to find His way

scripture 29

a defensive pattern of behavior can be
caused by abuse, or a sin against me
and i become protective of myself
and in so doing rejecting others or anyone else
that i perceive to do me harm
instead of letting God's strong arm
come to my defense and live in His love
not protectively, rather open to the above.

"...for the Lord your God is the one who goes with you.
He will not fail you or forsake you."

deuteronomy 31:6

scripture 30

"And now, Lord, for what do i wait? My hope is in You."

psalm 39:7

reminded i am of where my hope lies
in God alone though other things disguise
themselves as the answer to my solemn prayer
the Lord alone is the only place where
i can rest – and His hope is received
within throughout my very being
let me not wander away from Your path
for it is the only one that will last

the narrow
road...

scripture 150

"The Lord receives my prayer."

psalm 6:9

what a comfort it is to know
deep within, He loves me so
receiving any request i might make
or simple conversation, for heavens sake –
He receives my prayer, night and day
no matter silent or when i say
a plea, a thank you, He to hear
such a gift to know He is here.

scripture 189

"Now as they observed the confidence of peter and john and understood that they were uneducated and untrained men, they were amazed, and began to recognize them as having been with Jesus."

acts 4:13

are we recognized as having been?
with Jesus – how does your day begin?
do you celebrate your relationship with Thee
or is it really only secondary?
questions that each of us must ask ourselves
before ever pointing a finger at someone else
have i been in conversation
with my God or even meditation?
where has the day gone and who have i spent
my time with – has my posture been bent
in prayer, in reading of His word
have i heard His voice, what have i preferred?
there is no mystery in what i seek
may i confess that i am weak
and start anew, right now to choose
to be with You —

scripture 75

"i will be satisfied with Your likeness when i awake."

psalm 17:15b

Your likeness when i awake
above, Your countenance to not forsake
illumination that rises up from the grave
every morningtide, a reminder that You save
and i to be satisfied in Your truth portrayed
across the horizon, Your wisdom parades.

scripture 88

"But the fruit of the Spirit is love, joy, peace, patience,
kindness, goodness, faithfulness, gentleness, self-control.
against such things there is no law."

galatians 5:22 and 23

are not the fruit of His Spirit an echoing
of His presence to those around – we bring
His body no longer here to reside
and until His return "His body" to abide
within each of us who claim His name
and our fortune is to pour out His fame
in loving kindness and faithfulness that endure
with joy and patience in all our words
self control, gentleness, goodness, endowed
portrayed through good deeds and somehow
those that receive will be at peace –
visited by His freedom that provides release.

scripture 426

*"i wait for the Lord, my soul does wait and
in His word do i hope."*

psalm 130:5

in the darkened hours of the night
and also the dawn before first light

i wait for the Lord

when my heart aches and breaks again
i bow in prayer, my words to send

i wait for the Lord

daily as chaos makes itself known
another caller crying on the phone

i wait for the Lord

in thought and mediation for understanding
unaware of His future planning

i wait for the Lord

and when i wait my soul at rest –
kind and loving He does address

my need —

scripture 418

"For My flesh is true food, and My blood is true drink."

john 6:55

a meal to be given in His name
to remember His death 'til He comes again
a meal of bread and wine for we
accept His sacrifice, now on the family tree
a meal divine, our hunger satisfied
and in that moment His presence alive
a meal meager though to be
held within the Spirit of Thee

bread &

scripture 421

Then the Lord spoke to moses saying, "Command the sons of israel that they bring to you clear oil from beaten olives for the light to make a lamp burn continually."

leviticus 24:1-2

to the east upon the mount of olives was He
when He ascended in to heaven, for them to see
a perpetual light until He to return
every detail scripted and we are to learn
that nothing was happenstance, but foretold
in the scriptures long long ago –
all to be fulfilled at the time and place
that He ordained through His mercy and grace

scripture 540

"O send out Your light and Your truth let them lead me; let them bring me to Your holy hill and to Your dwelling places."

psalm 43:3

what a delightful prayer before dawn arrives
to send out Your light and truth for my stride
to lead me and bring me to Your holy hill
camping there in mornings still
Your dwelling places, that You've prepared
i believe we're to meet You there
and when we do such peace received
bountiful blessings, we believe

scripture 541

*"for the Holy Spirit will teach you in that very hour
what you ought to say."*

luke 12:12

no need for fretting or that we'll forget
in triumph and through His Spirit a defense
will be given in the exact hour
by His amazing and silent power
for it is not me, but His residence within
that i am reminded and strengthened to give
whatever words necessary and so to be held
in His precious and tender hands

scripture 10

"is that not what the showers meant
the rain that poured out above our heads."

psalm 148:4

were the heavens actually giving praise
ah – perhaps to look at the rain that way
nature to speak, Lord may we understand
as we read Your word, it be the sand
that You have written in, to comprehend
the wonder and glory that You send.

scripture 571

"So when it was evening on that day, the first day
of the week, and when
the doors were shut where the disciples were for
fear of the jews, Jesus came and stood
in their midst and said to them,
'peace be with you.'"

john 20:19

with eventide approaching He made His way
into the upper room where the disciples stayed –
bringing peace, the first words that He'd spoken
perhaps in silent prayer and now the stillness broken
what i find that is very interesting to me –
His focus on forgiveness , forever to be
the reason He came so that we might be
forgiven, our sins nailed to calvary's tree
before easter day became easter night
He wanted them to remember what was right
no darkness to invade, but when to shine
forgiveness was to be the anthem divine

scripture 209

"for a spirit of harlotry has led them astray."

hosea 4:12b

wow could He have been any more direct
the words above for us to detect
where we have veered from the road
turned off, gone our own way we're told
and by so doing our unfaithfulness
has drawn us into whoredom and nothing else
a dead end, that held promise at the time
only too late to realize and find

the truth —

scripture 210

"Arise, shine; for your light has come, And
the glory of the Lord has risen upon you."

isaiah 60:1

every day this mantra to repeat
as morningtide appears, the sunrise sweet
off to complain for needed is more sleep,
but the Son is calling us to our feet
to be awake, in silent prayer
and then to arise for He meets us there
upon my countenance He to shine
so others may see His glory divine

scripture 211

"for we are his workmanship created in Christ Jesus..."
ephesians 2:10

what everyday before the mirror we donned
this picture of glory laid upon
ourselves as His children,
to not be denied
and we in His glorious arrangement would
testify
to the wonder of His love, in which we're
embraced
how then would our days be graced
as His wonders to unfold —

scripture 212

"I shall make mention of the lovingkindnesses of the Lord,
the praises of the Lord."

isaiah 63:7a

His hesed love unable to comprehend
only to receive in and perhaps then to lend
to others who have yet to conceive
of the power of LOVE when within to receive
for when it consumes our very being
our personhood becomes about others seeing
His countenance, His acceptance of another
each made in His image amazing others
as our brothers

scripture 565

"and their sin I will remember no more."

*"For I will be merciful to their iniquities and
I will remember their sins no more."*

so important to remember and yet we forget
or refuse to believe for perhaps we get
muddled, confused, unwilling to accept
the freedom we receive, the joy that should let
us dance in the street, rejoice continually
for the Lord our God has forgiven thee,
but our guilt is a restraint that remains
instead of the love thats held by His name!

scripture 241

can we continually be aware
of His favorable presence – His love, His care?

can we allow ourselves to receive
accepting His love so that we can be…?

vessels of mercy, His promises fulfilled
to live in the grace of His perfect will

by His Spirit to wholly depend
on His living water to flow and when

we do, HIS trustworthy life
will be the wonder amidst the strife…

"…mercy trumps over judgment."

james 2:13

scripture 256

"...In holy array from the womb of dawn."

psalm 110:3b

what a splendid scripture to portray
Your birthday in bethlehem on that day –
from out of the darkness and into the light
the shepherds came to such delight
praising and glorifying Your heavenly Father
for all they had seen – and ever after –
perhaps being missionaries in the pasture lands
for was that not part of Your plan?

inspired by
luke 2:15-20

scripture 346

"For indeed in this house we groan longing to be clothed
with our dwelling from heaven."

II corinthians 5:2

ah is this not the cry of a mother who has lost a son
to be with him now…for that day to come
yet many days will pass for that day to be
together once again in eternity
the only solace one can take comfort from
it will only be a wink of an eye for the son
for time in eternity is not the same as here
so he is not alone for the Lord his God is near –

scripture 213

"So jehoiachin changed his prison clothes
and had his meals in the king's presence regularly all
the days of his life."

jeremiah 52:33

when the prison garments we lay aside
out of the tomb to celebrate our lives
given to us by the King of Kings
we sit at His table and wonderful things
become a reality in our lives as we allow ourselves to abide
receiving, accepting the new life given
our daily needs are met from the hands of heaven

scripture 214

to receive His love and to understand
there's an acceptance, an adoption that stands
it cannot be diminished or set aside
but we do need to fully abide
and when we do a confidence assured
a holy kind of discernment learned
as time passes day out and day in
a finer completion of His life within.

..."So the people without understanding are ruined."
hosea 4:14b

scripture 221

it's amazing how one can open wide
the word of God and to your own surprise
you fall upon a verse – exactly the morsel to feed
one's wearied soul, time and again received
for all knowing is the Father above
and like a mother bird feeding her love
to her chicks within the nest
my God and Father does His very best
to keep me alive

scripture 215

"The words of the wise heard in quietness
are better than the shouting of a ruler among fools."

ecclesiastes 9:17

is this not an encouragement to pray
for our country on any given day
in quietness to lift our concerns
and then perhaps those who rule to learn
Your ways my God and not to lean
On what they think or what has been
but rather by Your Spirit directed
inspired yet undetected –
ah the fate of our country now at stake
help us not to hesitate
rather on our knees to You alone
in quietness our request before the throne,

amen

"Trust in the Lord with all your heart And do not lean on
your own understanding. In all your ways acknowledge Him.
And He will make your paths straight."

proverbs 3:4-5

scripture 566

*"God is in the midst of her she will not be moved
God will help her when morning dawns."*

psalm 46:5

how often; daily, i find this to be true
from dark to light, morningtide blue
all worries, and concern seems to have melted away
with the light of dawn for He is in the day
though trouble may arrive or soon to come
in the midst He is and when day is done
i remember that He is with me still
through the dark of night i command His will
til morning once again is revealed
for in the light my hope is sealed

scripture 67

is this not a description of mornings tide
how deep, how strong, how wonderfully wide
that fills the dawn are we dulled to recognize
it is the God of Israel before our eyes –
brought before us, reminded we are to be
of His glorious intention for you and me
out of ephesians He predestined us for adoption
as sons
through Jesus Christ, His only begotten Son
the kindness of His will to the praise of the glory
of His grace freely bestowed, the salvation story

scripture 45

i remember that moment so grateful am i
to tell of my betroval and to testify
no longer orphaned or abandon i be
but rather joined in matrimony
to the Holy Groom, the King i adore
His name is Jesus – and forever more
i'll be His bride and my husband He'll be
for now, and forever in eternity

*"And i will betroth you to Me in faithfulness.
Then you will know the Lord."*

hosea 2:20

"He who separates himself seeks his own desire."

proverbs 18:1a

scripture 172

*"...just as Christ also loved you and gave
Himself up for us, an offering and a sacrifice
to God as a fragrant aroma."*

ephesians 5:2

as He hung on the cross – a perfumed scent
was lifted up to heaven, by His crucifixion sent
a sacrifice of such magnitude unable to comprehend
the agony and the ecstasy at golgatha to attend –
Lord help me appropriate the offering that occurred
upon the mount of crucifixion and the love that's endured

scripture 203

*"Let us come before His presence with thanksgiving. let
us shout joyfully to Him with psalms."*

psalm 95:2

to not wait 'til i arrive on the celestial shore,
but here on earth, to worship and adore
the One whose presence i give thanks
in joyful songs and psalm to celebrate
God of mercy and Saviour of love
who came to ransom from above
leaving Your throne in paradise to be
the answer for our eternity

scripture 207

"Exalt the Lord our God and worship at His footstool;
Holy is He."

psalm 99:5

is His footstool not the horizon line
the seam between heaven and earth, the divine
a place of wonder when the sun to arise
or at the very moment of eventide
a silent occurrence, yet His glory seen
over and over since creation it has been
and we as His children at His footstool enthralled
by the majesty, the wonder, the beauty and awe.

sunsets

days end to say adieu
with songs filled with gratitude
for His relentless presence be
and into the night He's holding me
never to forsake, never to leave
a promise that's been given to you and me
sleep well as He silently pulls the shade
ever gently on what He's made

sunset 25

as the day darkens, we are reminded again
of our inherent position that of sin
confession our need before our repose
deliberate, honest, letting God know
we are aware, repentant and to accept
His forgiveness and then to be met
with an overwhelming love that blankets
our being
good night we say – blessed and freeing —

sunset 115

laid it so smoothly up above in the sky
sunsets colors, amazed was i
for never do i tire of the colors chosen
always a tapestry beyond humankind woven
and tonight, was no different, glorious beauty
simply stated – a gift not a duty
bestowed upon those that reside here
no other reason than to draw us near

sunset 299

the clouds have come to cool the day
eventide has also made its way
allowing the color of the sky to dim
the artistry is all by Him
no matter the changes that may occur
i know they've been spoken by His word
and we get to see the obedience of creation
to marvel at His incredible meditation

sunset 379

a heavenly gleam had appeared in the sky
the clouds alight, dazzled was i
by the wonder beyond the window glass
ever so glorious, but as usual, not to last
a treat for mankind, yet not to keep
like all on earth – to disappear a feat
that only the Lord performs to whet our
appetites
for the future and all of its delights
are yet to be

sunset 380

the moon was bright and oh so full
its beauty created awe to pull
us closer to our Creator, God
somehow, we have traveled oh so far
away
and He in His infinite wisdom creates
moments in which we celebrate
His genius and His wisdom – to draw us back
so in this momentary world there is no
lack
of His presence

sunset 381

a corn moon the weatherman had said
another said harvest so before i went to bed –
i went out on the deck and to my delight
observed the moon and its holy light

sunset 431

midnight blue He's painted the sky
such wonder that cannot be denied
so rich the color, as if wet paint
and it makes me wonder if the saints
above have midnight blue feet
for perhaps to wade into the deep
the then place above, oh to wait
such joy and love to celebrate

sunset 450

the ink of heaven their footsteps now
indelible are they and we somehow
can only imagine, like a newborn's footprint
on parchment recorded, just a glint
of our entry as we walk the midnight sky
freedom such freedom one day for you and i

sunset 711

the brilliant sunset covered the eventide sky
breathtakingly beautiful i stopped for a while
to receive His mercy, to let it soak in
this wondrous gift given by Him –
dispersed through the atmosphere seen through
the clouds –
pink, magenta – His glory out loud!
yet silent the sky, as were my tears –
oh, to worship – open to love free of fear!

sunset 740

the end of the day swiftly to spread
across the horizon – as i head for bed
darkened the sky, made to repose
will i take His direction? only God knows

sunset 791

the God of glory spread His banner on high
inflamed, it covered the night sky
such color to stop and to stare
at this feat of wonder and wonder where
He creates such unimaginable events
and then to His children they are sent
like His Son with arms open wide
the exhilarating splendor across the sky

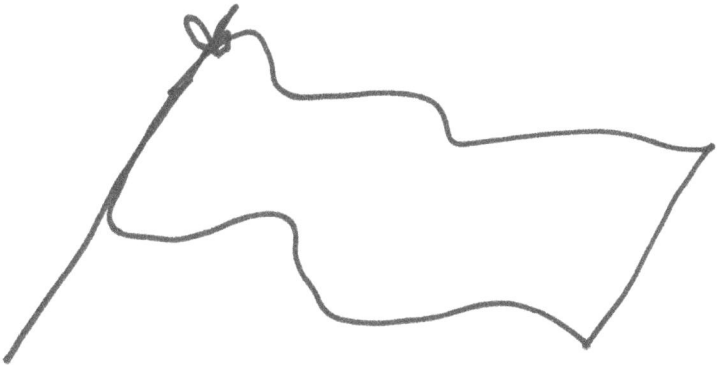

sunset 805

the color of blue that hung here below
the gates of paradise so that we'd know
just a glimpse of His throne room and its
glory
the royal blue sets the stage for His story
to just imagine the tapestries within
designed, measured, perhaps even hung by
Him –
await we do when the time will come –
before His throne and we to run
into His arms – return will we
into the eternal eden with Thee

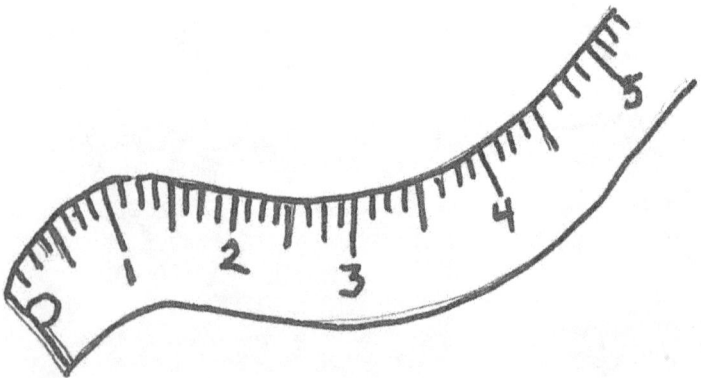

sunset 812

sunset had fallen without a sound
darkness soon after five pm all around
shorter days – perhaps more rest needed
the question is will it be heeded…
in His name Immanuel
His Incarnation celebrated well…
may it be

sunset 815

the sun to fall, the dark to fill
the sky as commanded by His will
now the moon held high, a lighted smile
as if a greeting – from so many miles
away – a silent salutation from His realm
and now in my heart held

sunset 825

the moon hung high; its light surprised
full it be – a beacon high –
our God's designs for day and night
wanting not to leave us without light

sunset 863

if gold had been poured from paradise's
front gates
across the eventide sky to celebrate
day's end and providing hope for the morrow
no matter life's regrets or evident sorrows
for He accompanies us on life's way
yesterday, tomorrow and yes for today

sunset 867

the still opened blinds i could see
the sun settling down, eventide to be
a slow glow burning in the sky
beautifully embered by my God and i
just watched as the flame to descend
the heavenlies were filled, held by the boughs to
send
a message of glory spread far and wide –
ever so lovely my God and His stride

sunset 868

so taken i was immersed in the glow
the tangerine and turquoise a beautiful show
to just sit and watch as night to arrive
hallowed the spectacle and i to abide
in the mystery —

sunset 873

the rooftops outlined in advent orange
sunset in the sky adorned
my evening and i was thrilled to see
the mystical beauty of my God tis Thee
that paints and arranges the heavenlies
i'm so amazed and over and over fall in love
drenched in His Presence, given from above.

sunset 888

to see the stars, a welcomed sight
surprised i was on this december night
long it had been since i have viewed
these lanterns, these illuminaries to amuse

sunset 942

the color of the sky is new to me
on this first day of 2018 and Thee
has thrilled my heart once again i say
for He's designed the nighttime by
His imagination, a full moon to spy
a globe so big and way up high
as if a hole poked in the velvet blue
to see the radiance of paradise beyond our view

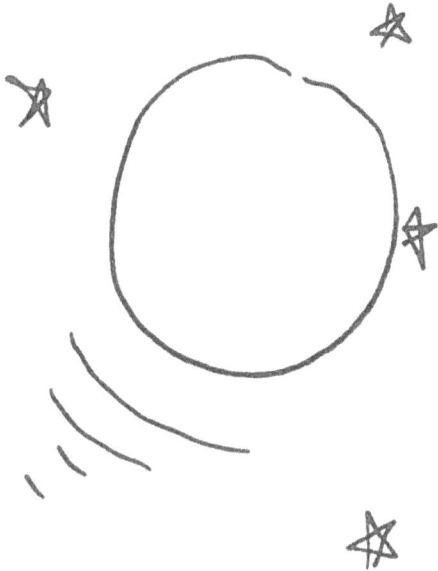

sunset 943

how am i guided by His light
In the darkest of day or the middle of night
where do i turn to be able to see
it's only when i look to Thee
a holy illumination is needed to be
through the Spirit my heart by Thee
is captured and only then to find
the sacred pathway i am now aligned
His word, the signposts we're to view
reading, taking in nourishment from You
and when upon the road we become
pilgrims, hopefully daughters and sons

amen

*Set your mind on the things above, not on the thing
that are on earth.*

colossians 3:2

sunset 406

bolts of satiny ribbon; the cloud formations
colored by the water held, a distinct celebration
at sunset the glory shone for miles
for everyone looking up to certainly bring smiles
purple, blue, scarlet, stained were the clouds
i felt as though the Lord speaking aloud
"look My children as seen the preview above
where one day the prepared place we will share with love."

sunset 408

spectacular was all i could continue to think
the clouds at sunset, oil painting pink
they swirled and filled; anointing the sky
breathtakingly beautiful the scene to spy
wondering and hoping that others too saw
the exquisite artwork and also the awe
that He had created, silently displayed
His workshop exposed – amazingly laid
for us to see.

sunset 448

the sunset spread so far and wide
golden was the eventide sky
glowing as though a forecast of the morrow –
an eternal glimpse to dismiss the sorrow
perspective to soothe the rage within
the chaos of life the wrath of sin
for the hope, that lies ahead
streets of gold – no more to be said

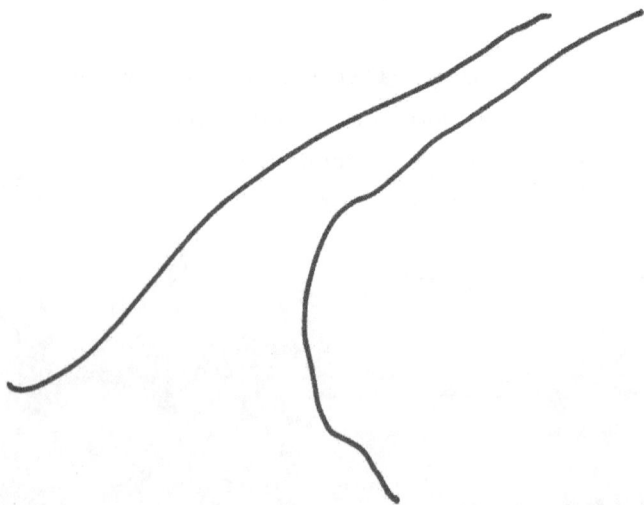

sunset 780

the beauty of the Lord dwelt at the horizon line tonight
a stunning shimmer spread across the sky quite a sight
its always a surprise the awe that surrounds
the presence of God – from the heavens to the ground
each season from winter to fall –
invites us to appreciate the Lord's call
often silent yet His whispers can be heard
in the crown of sunrise or the song of a bird
and like tonight an earnest glow
at the sky's hem, wanting us to know
we're in His thoughts.

sunset 787

days end from blue to gray
and then pitch – it is His way
from out of the dark rescued we be
into God's Son – daylight to see
salvation, resurrection out of the tomb
a new creation a second birth from the womb
of God

sunset 31

ever so slowly the embers of the day
sink and burn out and fade away
the sky now darkened midnight lights
stars in the heavens and though it night
there's a comfort knowing He's named each one
did they decide together the Father and Son?
calling to mind one day He'll call me
by the name that is only known by Thee

*"He who has an ear, let him hear what the
Spirit says to the churches.
To him who overcomes,
to him I will give some of the hidden manna,
and I will give him a white stone,
and a new name written on the stone
which no-one knows but he who receives it."*

revelation 2:17

sunset 42

i watch as eventide so gently falls
silently yet there is a call
headlights turn on, lamps alight
slowly from day into the night
much like sin when we enter in
a darkening as we stray from Him
we will watch and catch our fall
by His Spirit, we to recall
our Saviour

sunset 67

there are no words for the kindling that closed the day –
a fire so magnificent, the hearth of heaven some might say –
aflamed the sky – a holy spire
to set a tone, perhaps to inspire
each of us for the morrow to come
He to bequeath and we to run
into each new day with joy!

sunset 105

i'm watching and noting the hours to pass
as the daylight breathes its last breath
dusk; that time in between day and night
the dash, slowly edging out the light
a curtain to close, a drape to be dropped
every day – it not to be stopped
darkness can often elicit fear,
but better thought, rest to be near
so that in the hours to come light once again
would be applauded and welcomed in

sunset 108

i want to wait as long as i can
before lighting the lamps for when
turned on i'll not be as able to observe
the light outside as it dims so to serve
how i want to spend this time of eventide
perhaps a candle to be at my side
to patiently watch, a silent still
as the days face is veiled by His will
ever so slow – as an inside flame flickers
this time of year as day shortens we bicker
with God wanting longer illumination,
but the Father knows best and so days termination

"You appoint darkness and it becomes night..."
psalm 104:20

sunset 109

no fear in Jesus and so to see
the nightfall as a gift from Thee
as in the creation story to be told
there was an evening and morning – to unfold
the darkness lasted before the light
rest given to us in the night
not to be frightened rather rested to enter in
to each new day – let the day begin
another way to consider the deep blue
of the heavens not a scary hue,
but rather God's suggestion for repose
even in the time of day He wants us to know
His grace

sunset 150

moored to the God of eternity
for He's poured His love into me
and i am steadied by His abundance
within my soul, there's no redundance
only anticipation of His clever light
that appears most unexpectantly through
the night
and so i'm comforted, for no longer alone
His presence within my very bones.

sunset 205

embraced i am by tonight's eventide
wrapped around the moon and settled its stride
out my kitchen window, oh the shade of blue
the wings of a joy – a stunning hue
that if it had a sound would be played
by a symphony of violins, strongly laid
in unison upon the wind
a holy tribute sent by Him
my God and His wonders to never cease
glory and revelation – a good night's peace

sunset 222

at the end of the day there is an adieu
i believe created for me and you
like a candle flame to slowly dwindle
the torch of the day, no longer to kindle

rather into the ground only to stay
until of course the dawn of a new day
and rise it does, golden be the skies
a hope to come to testify

of resurrection from the grave
out of the darkness into the day
such wonder He wants us to know

sunset 227

eventide a lavender and blue sheer
had been hung over the hill
in the distance i watched the color
deepening –
as if the heavens above were weeping
and all through the night hours it rained
torrential at times and i wondered the drain
that sin has had upon the heavenlies
for it to rain so much indeed

sunset 22

eventide, the moon had been revealed
and yet the stars were still concealed
pale the sky, powdered the blue
i watched and dusk to view
a slow and quiet entry to night
and every day i witness the sight
to learn His pace and not my own
but rather the One upon the throne

"Bless the Lord, O my soul!
O Lord my God,
You are very great;
You are clothed with spender and majesty...

psalm 104:1

Thank You

i believe this book has been prayed for by many hearts. having written my first poem in 1998. the Lord, ever faithful, slowly created a group of listening ears that then encouraged me to continue to share His whispers.

First, the women in the monday morning bible study who have met for the last thirteen years. dani bradford, the hostess, has showed us such wonderful hospitality, and the nimble fingers of many of these gals typed all the poems. sue seline has led the charge, and i also want to thank her daughter casey seline who was a tremendous help. the support of this group has been invaluable.

there have been some friends who have been very financially supportive. i mention this because to "be silent and still" takes time. their help has maintained my budget and has produced a sweet grace so I needed not to be concerned. provision has been given by the following: craig and brenda nelson, dan and nancy edwards, arlene murphy, wes and patti mcbride, steve and lynette nabity, dave and kim nabity, sharon boll, and monday morning bible study.

there have also been many other friends who I have leaned over God's word with, such as all the women in "praying the scriptures" on thursday morning at St. Wenceslaus Catholic Church. the Holy Spirit has been with us and it has been such a wonderful experience to watch the poetry flow in this setting.

all the moms and dads who I have met through "a mother's hope" who have invited me into their grief have grown me in ways that i am forever grateful.

lisa pelto, when escorting me through the organization of this book for publication, suggested that i include those who encouraged me when I was younger. certainly, that would be mr. peter vogt and mr. thomas whippler, my seventh and eighth grade english teachers. they were excellent men who taught at shore junior high school in euclid, ohio.

over these forty-five years of being a child of God, i've had the privilege of being a member of a few churches from pennsylvania to ohio to nebraska. all of them have helped me to mature in the Lord. they are Riverview Presbyterian Church, Church of the Saviour, Trinity/Lifegate Interdenominational Church, and Coram Deo Church.

life has provided me with a marriage of forty years, three beautiful children, their spouses, and grandchildren that are a joy. The Lord has used all of this to bring me to this point. my life verse is Ephesians 2:10,

For we are His workmanship created in Christ Jesus for good works, which God prepared beforehand so that we would walk in them.

may you hear my Lord's voice and give Him thanks for He has made this book a reality and i am very grateful.

about the author

j. elizabeth sharon's deepest passion has been to know God and share His love and joy with others. after penning her first poem in 1998, she has no fewer than 35,000 poems gifted to her by God. a native of euclid, ohio, she has spent much of her life in omaha, nebraska leading bible studies and discipling women for the past 35 years. when she is not writing poetry from her kitchen table, she can be found painting with water colors, devouring her latest bookstore find or desiring time with her children and their families.

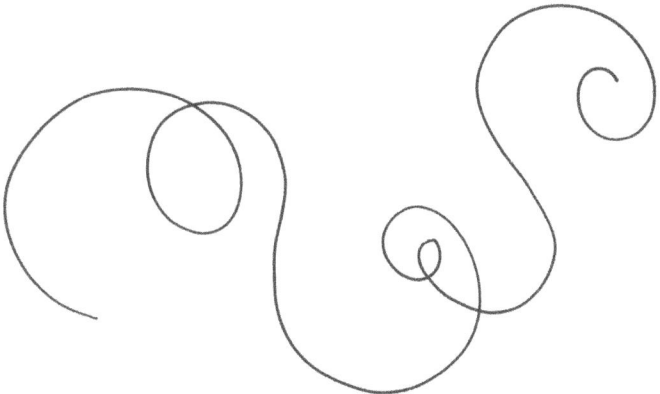

amen

* 9 7 8 1 9 4 5 5 0 5 3 6 2 *